I0016460

Contents

Introduction

The manufacturing planning process, at a high level, is outlined in the diagram below.

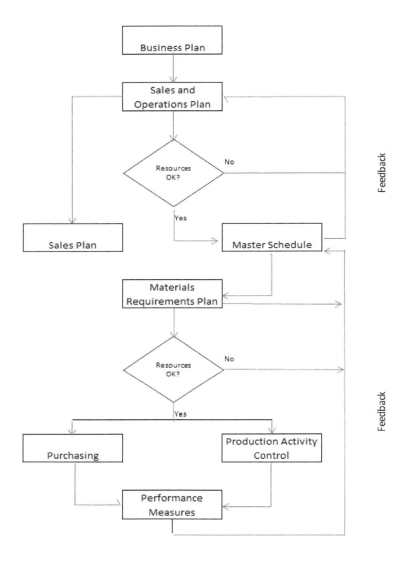

(Arnold & Chapman, 2004, p. 28)

In the diagram above, there are two primary decision points where the question "Do we have adequate resources?" is asked. The first is during the business planning stage, the second is during the production planning stage. However, this does not adequately address what an MRP II system is intended to accomplish. This is best stated in the form of a problem statement as follows:

> As forecasted demand changes, different demands are, in turn, placed on the labor, equipment and financial resources (i.e. investment in inventory) of the business. Decisions must be made as to what the best approach or approaches are to effectively address changing demand and the impact this has on the business.

These changes in forecasted demand occur at various stages of the planning cycle. In the business planning stage where long term planning and strategy are discussed. This stage would also address strategic options as it relates to capacity should the master production schedule (MPS) generated from the demand forecast indicate has or is about to become an area of concern. Otherwise capacity and equipment utilization decisions will be addressed at the MPS/operations level. From the perspective of master planning or shorter planning windows and day to day operations, reallocation of resources occur regularly as forecasted demand is replaced with actual customer orders. Schedules and the allocation of resources adjust accordingly.

In order to adequately address this problem statement, management uses a number of operations management techniques to establish various rules in the inventory management and production planning processes. The primary resources available to a manufacturer are material, equipment and labor. This paper will discuss the key rules and decisions involved in the following functions/processes within a manufacturing firm used to address this problem and ultimately answer the question, "Do we have adequate resources?":

> Inventory Management

> Forecasted Demand

> Production Planning

This paper will focus on inventory management and production planning decisions. It will be noted where other potential options are available to management where appropriate but will for all intents and purposes be beyond the scope of this paper.

Process Strategy

Before delving into the specific components of MRP II systems, an overall framework for the processes under which the manufacturing firm operates should be established. This relates to the nature of the demand for the firms finished product: whether or not volumes are high or low and; how much variability there is in the types of products manufactured. There are four main process strategies employed by manufacturers that determine not only how an operation is physically set up but how inventory is managed, transacted and planned. These are:

➢ Process Focused – characterized by small quantities and a large variety of products

➢ Repetitive Focused – characterized by standardized products with added options or features

➢ Product Focused – characterized by large volumes and low variety of products

➢ Mass Customization – characterized by large volumes and a large variety of products (Heizer & Render, 2006, pp. 256-260)

Determining which strategy best fits the manufacturers operation, will also determine how product is scheduled. For example, when quantities are small but the variety of products is large, this implies that it may be more appropriate to make finished product to order rather than make to a forecast and store because finished stock may be in inventory for longer periods waiting for customer orders increasing inventory carrying costs. A repetitive focused strategy implies that component parts can be built ahead of time awaiting further assembly once the additional features have been determined. Depending on demand, it may be appropriate to make to order or make to forecast and store. For a product focused strategy product can be made to a forecast and stored because the variety of products is low and volumes are large. This implies that production schedules can be adjusted up or down as actual demand becomes known and forecasts are adjusted without incurring substantial inventory carrying costs (make to forecast) because of the relatively small number of SKUs. Mass customization would obviously be made to order as features cannot be known in advance but the manufacturing process itself must be very flexible to accommodate the high frequency of changeovers.

The volume and variety of products manufactured will determine whether inventory transactions are batched and what the optimum batch sizes are or if they should be recorded as a continuous flow. This has implications for capacity from the frequency of changeovers necessary to meet demand from an extreme of no or very few changeovers in a continuous flow or product focused environment to many changeovers in a process focused one.

Components of MRP II

Inventory Management

At the core of production planning is inventory management. This paper will concern itself with three primary categories of inventory that are directly related to the manufacturing process: raw materials, work in progress and finished goods.

> "Inventories are materials and supplies that a business or institution carries either for sale or to provide inputs or supplies to the production process. All businesses and institutions require inventories….. Inventory management is responsible for planning and controlling inventory from the raw material stage to the customer. Since inventory either results from production or supports it, the two cannot be managed separately and, therefore, must be coordinated." (Arnold & Chapman, 2004)

Inventories are the mechanism by which a manufacturer manages fluctuations in customer orders and move through the production process in either a continuous flow or in batches depending on the size and variability of customer demand patterns. As previously stated, if demand is relatively stable and of a large enough quantity, it may be justifiable to set up dedicated production lines to manufacture product in a continuous flow. If demand is variable and/or in small quantities, manufacturers may choose to produce in batch quantities that are determined based on a calculated minimum cost effective quantity. Inventory management has three main goals which are often in conflict with one another:

> Maximize customer service levels

> Minimize cost of production

> Minimize inventory investment (Arnold & Chapman, 2004, p. 240)

For example, in order to maximize customer service levels firms will want to maintain high inventory levels in order to meet customer order demand and minimize the risk of a stock out. Carrying large amounts of inventory however has several costs associated with it. Minimizing the cost of production involves increasing batch sizes or operating in a continuous flow which can result in increased inventory levels and increased carrying costs.

The costs associated with the production and stocking of inventory include:

> Cost to purchase – cost of the item itself, transportation

> Carrying costs – warehousing, obsolescence, pilferage, capital costs

> Ordering costs – purchasing department, production control department,

> Stock-out costs – running out of inventory and loss of associated sale or customer, back-order costs

> Capacity-associated costs – set-up and tear-down costs (Arnold & Chapman, 2004, pp. 240-243)

The primary concern of inventory management is to balance the three competing priorities by carrying the optimum inventory levels that minimize the costs of carrying inventory while at the same time maximizing customer service levels and minimizing production costs. To do this management defines rules by which inventory is to be managed to determine:

- ➤ What to buy – bills of materials or recipes are defined and outline what quantity of raw material and/or work in process is required to produce a given quantity of finished good.

- ➤ When to buy it – purchasing lead times, manufacturing lead times (as defined by set up times and run times) determine when raw materials and work in process items are needed for input into the next stage of the manufacturing process in order to satisfy demand.

- ➤ How much to buy – also determined by the bill of materials but also by minimum order quantities defined either by the supplier or minimum economic order quantities as determined by the firms carrying and ordering costs.

- ➤ How much to keep on hand – determined by the firms carrying costs, purchasing and/or manufacturing lead times, customer order demand

- ➤ What to make – determined by actual customer order volume and/or forecasted customer orders

- ➤ When to make it – determined by customer requested delivery dates and /or forecasted customer orders, the need to replenish safety stocks (how much to keep on hand).

In order to achieve these goals, control over in inventory is realized through the establishment of stock keeping units or SKUs. (Arnold & Chapman, 2004) Each item is given its own SKU identification. In order to determine when a new SKU identification is needed, the rule of form-fit-function (FFF) should apply. Form-fit-function is a "grouping of fully interchangeable parts that are identical in all of their technically relevant properties." (SAP) FFF eliminates any question as to whether or not one SKU is interchangeable with another. However, as products and customer requirements evolve, what does not constitute a new SKU today may require a new SKU tomorrow. When considering the establishing of a new SKU, by not establishing multiple SKUs for what is essentially the same thing, a firm is in a better position to realize the goal of optimizing inventory levels while minimizing production and holding/carrying costs by not having an additional SKU for which to maintain stock and to not have separate bills of material and routings (work instructions) required to produce or to consume an additional SKU.

SKU Records

The SKU record contains information to assist the firm with managing and controlling inventory. The fields in the SKU record interact with planning and scheduling applications or modules or aid in reporting and controlling inventory levels. Some of this information, along with the SKU identifier or number and description, includes:

- ➢ Safety Stock – determined by management based on demand and lead times.
- ➢ Quantity on Hand – determined by inventory transactions
- ➢ Available to Promise – function of quantity on hand, the planning window, customers requested delivery date, production orders
- ➢ Make or Buy – determined by management
- ➢ ABC Code – used in planning to determine which inventories to plan and to what level of control
- ➢ Purchasing Lead Time – defined by the supplier
- ➢ Manufacturing Lead Time – typically calculated by the primary routing
- ➢ Product Class – typically identifies whether a SKU is a raw material, intermediate or finished good. Typically has significance in directing transactional activity in the accounting system and may or may not facilitate planning.

- Product Subclass – further distinguishes product categories. May or may not have significance in directing transactional activity in the accounting system and may or may not facilitate planning.

- Minimum Order Quantity – can be designated by the supplier or by the manufacturer consuming.

- Economic Order Quantity – calculated taking into consideration inventory demand, ordering and carrying costs.

- Unit of Measure – the weight, volume or linear measure that denotes the measurement that quantities on hand and available relate to for a given SKU (for example, kilogram, square metre, litre, each, etc.)

- Primary Bills of Material (costing and manufacture – we will only be concerned about manufacture for purposes of this paper)

- Primary Routing (costing and manufacture – we will only be concerned about manufacture for purposes of this paper)

Inventory Accuracy

Although warehousing and distribution are beyond the scope of this paper, it should be mentioned that these functions play a critical role within the supply chain function. One function, its contribution to accurate inventory records, is critically important to ensure that the results of any production planning system generates can be relied upon. In order to ensure inventory is as accurate as possible, inventory transactions should be recorded as close to source as possible. This means that when inventory is physically moved, produced or consumed, the transaction representing this event should be recorded as timely as possible. Delays in recording transactions from the time they physically occur can increases the chance or error or can be forgotten and not recorded at all. It may also have an impact when someone in the warehouse or production is looking for a SKU and it is not where the inventory system indicates it should be located or it is there but not in the quantity indicated in the inventory record.

Consideration should also be given to the physical layout of the warehouse in terms of ease of picking and put-away, the nature of the inventory to determine the most appropriate infrastructure for storage as well as requirements for staging and sorting in preparation for shipping. (Frazell, New York, p. 8) To ensure accurate inventory records, attention also needs to be paid to SKU demand patters. (Frazell, New York, p. 30)

Forecasting Demand and Planning

Demand Forecast

The next component of the Manufacturing Resource Planning (MRPII) system is the demand forecast.

> "Demand forecasts are projections of demand for a company's products or services. These forecasts, also called sales forecasts, drive a company's production, capacity, and scheduling systems…. Good forecasts are of critical importance in all aspects of a business: The forecast is the only estimate of demand until actual demand becomes known." (Heizer & Render, 2006, p. 107)

There are several methodologies that can be used in estimating demand but the end result is that the business has a picture of:

➢ What SKUs they need to produce

➢ The quantities of each SKU

➢ The timing of when the demand needs to be filled (i.e. which calendar month)

Armed with this information, the manufacturer can determine, in conjunction with available inventories what the forecasted pattern of production and purchasing will be for the time horizon of the forecast. To do this, the company uses what's referred to as bills of material to calculate all of the components required to make the forecasted quantities of end products in the forecast. In addition, by using those same forecasted quantities, inventory levels and what's known as routings it can be determined what the demand will be on production capacity (i.e. how much time will be required on each piece of equipment in the manufacturing facility and when that machine time will be required). With these two pieces of information it can be determined if any additional build of inventory will be required by manufacturing intermediate or finished goods SKUs ahead of forecasted demand when demand exceeds the firms' ability to produce. This may also require that additional raw materials be acquired as well.

Manufacturing Resource Planning

Manufacturing resource planning (MRP II) systems include master planning, capacity planning and materials planning. MRP II is itself defined as "a method for the effective planning of all resources of a manufacturing company." (Arnold & Chapman, 2004, p. 27)

In order to effectively plan manufacturing operations certain master data must be present and include:

- ➢ A demand forecast
- ➢ Inventory master – these are the identified raw material, intermediate, and finished good SKUs and contains information as previously noted in the SKU record section.
- ➢ Work Centers and Machines
    - o Work Centers – a group of similar machines for purposes of determining production capacity.
    - o Machine – a unit used in determining production capacity
- ➢ Warehouse and Location Master – warehouse locations and bin locations within the warehouse representing where inventory items can be physically located within the warehouse.

➤ Bills of Materials – the recipe or listing, with quantities, necessary to manufacture a given quantity of an item.

➤ Routings – the work instructions including the machine, set up time, run time necessary to manufacture a given quantity of an item

➤ Calendar – this sets when the equipment is available for use including days of the week and hours. It also incorporates any planned shutdowns and holidays, if applicable, when equipment will not be available for use. It is used in conjunction with shifts.

➤ Shift – when shifts start and end. When used in conjunction with the calendar it will determine if equipment will be available, for example 24 hours per day, 7 days per week or only 12 hours per day, 5 days per week or some other combination.

➤ Vendor Master and Vendor Item Cross Reference – for purchased or "buy" items, the vendor item cross reference is a record that identifies which vendor supplies which items to the manufacturing firm. Where there are multiple vendors that supply a given item, each one may have their own lead times. This may be specified here and over-ride the information residing in the item master.

➤ Unit of Measure Conversion – often items can be purchased or sold in multiple units of measure. In order for the system to understand and translate the quantities, unit of measure conversion records are set up to translate, for example, how many pounds equate to a kilogram or how many grams are in a kilogram etc.

Bills of Material

A bill of material (BOM) is a "…listing of all the subassemblies, intermediates, parts, and raw materials that go into a parent assembly showing the quantity of each required to make an assembly. It is used in conjunction with the master production schedule to determine the items for which purchase requisitions and production orders must be released." (APICS The Association for Operations

Management, 2010, p. 13)   The bill of material draw on information from the item master, inventory quantities available, unit of measure conversions, the warehouse and location master data and the demand forecast to determine what volume of the component quantities are necessary to produce a given quantity of a finished SKU.

Routings

A routing describes how a SKU is manufactured. Routings "... include the operations be performed, their sequence, the various work centres involved, and the standards for setup and run." (i.e. setup times and run times. Routings use information stored in the work centre, machine master, inventory master, inventory quantities available, shift master data, demand forecast and the calendar to determine how long it will take to make a given quantity of a finished SKU.

Master Production Schedules

A master production schedule (MPS) is "...what the company plans to produce in specific configurations, quantities and dates.... takes into account the forecast, the production plan and other important considerations such as backlog, availability of material, availability of capacity and management policies and goals." (APICS The Association for Operations Management, 2010, p. 88) Depending on the timing of forecast demand or customer orders, it may be necessary to make product ahead of the time to eliminate bottleneck areas within the production process. The master production schedule provides a high level view of the operation and provides information to assist with decisions to be made with respect to inventory levels, potential insight into additional equipment investment that may be necessary to eliminate bottlenecks or customer pricing decisions to better manage demand where demand exceeds capacity (increasing prices) or there is excess capacity in the system (lowering prices).

The overall process can be summarized in the following diagram:

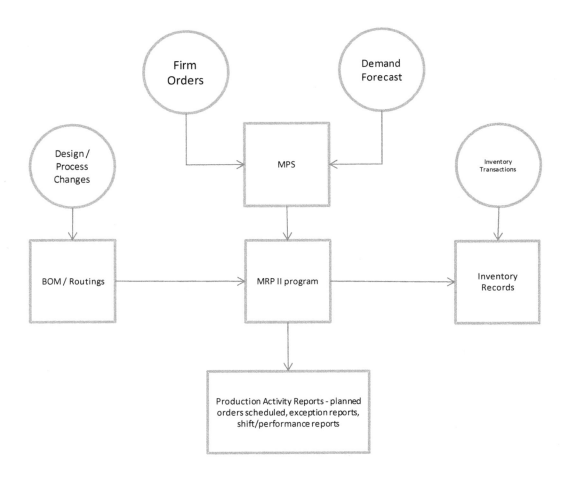

(Chase, Shankar, Jacobs, & Aquilano, 2011, p. 692)

Capacity Planning and Bottlenecks

A bottleneck machine is a machine that has a demand placed on it that is exceeds its capacity. (APICS The Association for Operations Management, 2010) The entire network of equipment cannot produce an amount that exceeds the capacity of the bottleneck machine or work centre. This is where capacity planning comes into play as inventory of intermediate components or even finished goods can be produced in advance to compensate for constraints placed on the system by bottlenecks. As previously mentioned, inventory is not the only option at managements' disposal; selling price can also be used to manage demand. Raising and lowering prices may not be such a simple task depending on the market in which a firm operates or because of contractual obligations that the firm has with its customers. Management may have to decide whether or not to accept an order based on its profitability.

Decision Rules and the Decision Process

As you can see, there are many variables that can come into play that determine how much product a manufacturer can produce and when. Depending on the complexity of the manufacturing process and the number of volume of SKUs that need to be produced, this can be done manually but as complexity increases computerized systems are required.

To illustrate consider a forecasted demand for a finished SKU (FG1), inventory levels for FG1 and raw material components (RM1 and RM2) and the following scenario:

Forecasted Demand

SKU	Quantity
FG1	500

Inventory

SKU	Quantity on Hand	Quantity Available	Purchasing Lead time (days)
FG1	100	100	N/A
RM1	50	50	2
RM2	200	200	7

Machines

Machine	Output Rate/hr	Shifts
M1	10	24 hours/7 days/52 weeks

Order Date:	August 1, 2012
Request Date:	August 10, 2012

The following bill of materials and routings represent how SKU FG1 is produced and the rate (in units per hour) at which machine M1 can produce FG1. For simplicity of illustration, it is assumed that there is no set up time, that a process focused strategy is employed, no safety stock is typically maintained for this SKU and that the batch was determined to be 100. Assuming that there is no other demand, the August 10 delivery date

Bill of Material (assume batch size of 100)

SKU Produced	Quantity
FG1	100

SKU Consumed	Quantity
RM1	80
RM2	20

Routing

Machine	Rate/hr
M1	10

In order to satisfy this demand, 400 units of FG1 will have to be produced (demand – quantity available = 500 -100 = 400). This will take 40 hours or just under 2 days (demand / rate per hour = 400 / 10 = 40). However, component inventory levels need to be taken into consideration as well. In order to produce 400 units of FG1 we will require 320 units of RM1 (80 X 4) and 80 units of RM2 (20 X 4). Upon reviewing the inventory we have adequate inventory of RM2 but will have to place an order with a supplier in order to have the necessary inventory on hand to produce FG1 (we need to order 270 units of RM1). With an order lead time of 2 days and assuming todays date is August 1, we will have the raw material on hand to make the FG1 to satisfy the order by August 3. With 2 days to manufacture we have enough inventory of FG1 on hand on August 5. Assuming that 5 days is enough time to ship the product for it to arrive at the customer's location, we will be able to manufacture the SKU and satisfy the demand. If the rate per hour on machine M1 was lower, perhaps 4 units and the purchasing lead time on raw material was 10 days it would have taken 100 hours or 4 days to produce the order but we would not have been able to start production until the component RM was received on August 11; the day after the customer wanted to receive the order. In this case, we would not have been able to satisfy the demand. The customer would either have had to accept a later delivery date or seek an alternate supplier. The process flow that is supported by the demand forecast, inventory, bills of material and routing is illustrated below:

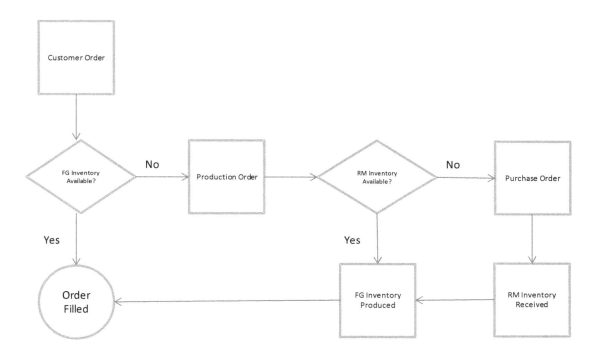

If, in the scenario outlined, the demand changes from 500 to 1000, the firm's ability to meet the demand may or may not be impacted. Manufacturers are not often dealing with one piece of equipment and one order for one SKU but products often require processing through several pieces of equipment all with varying output rates with different raw materials and intermediate components being produced and consumed at each stage. Moreover, it is not one SKU with one request date but several, perhaps hundreds of SKUs with different quantities and request dates for delivery to various destinations. A simple linear algebra equation suddenly becomes much more complicated.

The field of operations management employs a number of techniques to assist in managing competing priorities and aid in guiding the decision process to drive improvements in achieving objectives of the three main goals of inventory management: lower carrying costs, lower production costs, higher customer service levels. Some of these decision rules include but are not limited to:

➢ Forecasting accuracy

➢ Safety Stock Levels – minimize the risk of stock-outs while attempting to satisfy the competing goals of minimizing inventory levels and maximizing customer service levels.

➢ Planning Horizon – to narrow a planning horizon may result in out of stock situations or excessive stock to wide a planning horizon may cause a higher number of scheduling changes as the demand forecast is replaced by actual orders.

➢ Batching (and associated batch size) or continuous operation – batch sizes that are to large may make machines more efficient but result in excessive inventory builds, to small and machines become less efficient and the risk of stock-outs increases.

➢ Customer service level – perhaps on time deliveries as measured by actual delivery vs. customer request date

Operations Management Techniques and Measuring Performance

Demand Forecasting

Since the demand forecast is a crucial input into the MRP II system, a great deal of research has been done to determine the best methodology. Unfortunately, it is often the case that the best method to use cannot be determined until after the actual demand becomes known. This makes demand forecasting a process of trial and error. (Lofti & Pegels, 1996) There are five main quantitative forecasting methods:

> Naïve approach – the least sophisticated. It assumes that the forecast for the coming month will equal the actual results of the prior month. In the absence of data to project volumes, this is as good an approach as any.

> Moving averages –takes the average of a number of months as determined by the forecaster and uses that as the basis for projecting future months.

> Exponential Smoothing – applies a smoothing factor as determined by the forecaster against the forecast error from the prior month and adds this to the prior month forecast to arrive at the forecast for the coming month.

> Trend Projections – users the least squares method against historical demand to determine the trend line in demand

> Linear Regression - analyzes historical data in correlation with external factors such as overall economic conditions and the overall competitive landscape and future economic forecasts can provide some insight into future demand patterns. (Heizer & Render, 2006, pp. 109-133)

Firms can also, collaborate with business customers and share information on required volumes. The benefit of this greater visibility for the customer is that it can provide stability in their supply chain. Contractual arrangements can aid in smoothing demand patterns. There is no one best forecasting methodology. What provides accurate forecasting now may not in the future as other variables come into play that either favorably or unfavorably affects demand.

Chase, Shankar, Jacobs and Aquilano assert that Box Jenkins and Shiskin Time Series provide more accurate overall demand and demand patterns. (Chase, Shankar, Jacobs, & Aquilano, 2011, p. 553) but demand can be affected by numerous factors and as the competitive landscape changes and markets evolve, adjustments to whatever model or models are selected will still need to be made. To compensate for this, different forecasting methodologies can be used. Hugos asserts that by doing so, better forecasting accuracy can be achieved than by relying on one method alone. (Hugos, 2006, p. 52)

Measuring Forecast Error

There are several methods for measuring forecast error but one of the more popular is Mean Absolute Deviation (MAD) and calculated as the absolute value of the average deviation from forecast. (Chase, Shankar, Jacobs, & Aquilano, 2011, p. 566) With forecasting accuracy of such high importance to the results generated from MRP II systems, measuring actual variances to forecast and adjusting forecasting methodologies accordingly is an important activity however much of the literature indicates that determining optimal forecast figures is often done offline using other application, particularly Excel, implying that only the end results are entered in the planning system. This is potentially an opportunity for improvement particularly for those industries with volatile markets or time sensitive supply chains.

Inventory Management - ABC Classifications

This technique determines the importance of each inventory item and categorizes them into an ABC classification. Given that, as already discussed, carrying inventory has a cost associated with it, it follows that. A items account for 80% of the investment in inventory and should have the tightest controls including regular review of quantities on hand, frequent review of demand forecasts and active management of lead times. C items account for 5% of the investment in inventory but the most number of items, they should have the lowest controls and could include periodic cycle or physical counts or be managed through Kanban (a visual inventory pull system where cards are placed in bins indicating the re-order point has been reached and purchasing needs to be notified (APICS The Association for Operations Management, 2010, p. 77)). B items would have "normal" controls with periodic review of quantities on hand and demand forecast but not with the same rigor as A items.

- A – up to 20% of the items account for up to 70% of the dollar usage

- B – up to 20% of the items account for up to 20% of the dollar usage

- C – up to 60% of the items account for 10-30% of the dollar usage (APICS The Association for Operations Management, 2010, p. 1)

The percentages are rules of thumb but the principle is that A, B and C items are planned and managed in inventory differently depending on the demand pattern of the SKUs in each category and the process strategy employed.

Inventory Management – Inventory Levels and Batch Sizes

Two formulas have been established to determine the maximum inventory level and batch size and they are :

(Maximum Inventory Levels) $I_M = \sqrt{(2DS / H)} \times \sqrt{((P - D) / P)}$

and

(Maximum Batch Size) $Q^* = \sqrt{(2DS / H)} \times \sqrt{(P / (P - D)}$

Where:

D is the annual demand in units

S is the machine set up cost

H is the inventory holding cost

P is the annual production rate in units per year (Lofti & Pegels, 1996, p. 323)

Inventory turnover

Represents the number of times inventory is replenished over a given period of time, typically a year. (APICS The Association for Operations Management, 2010, p. 74) Management can establish policies on inventory turnover overall or on the various categories of inventory (raw material, work in process/intermediate and finished goods).

Productivity

Built into the routings, are productivity rates for every manufactured SKU or rate at which the SKU is produced. As plant orders are completed, actual results can be evaluated against the routing targets or standards and corrective actions taken if necessary. Management can also establish targets for productivity improvements either by reducing set up times or modifications to work process than improve run times.

Equipment Utilization

Equipment utilization is the ratio of actual equipment usage to the amount of time it is available for use. (APICS The Association for Operations Management, 2010, p. 159) This measure used in conjunction with productivity measurements, determine the capacity of the operation. Equipment utilization, a function of time if measured in isolation from productivity may provide a distorted measure if a department slows a piece of equipment down to match the demand level. However, utilization measured in conjunction with productivity will make such an occurrence obvious.

Potential Shortcomings of MRP II

Business systems have evolved from the 1960's where they were accounting systems to the integrated ERP systems we see today.

Accounting Systems $\rightarrow$ + Inventory Control and Purchasing $\rightarrow$ MRP $\rightarrow$ MRP II $\rightarrow$ ERP

However, as sophisticated as MRP II and ERP systems are they have their shortcomings; according to Gumaer, MRP II systems cannot "... meet the need to plan, execute, and redirect manufacturing process in real time." (Gumaer, 1996, p. 33). This need is emerging from the changing landscape of business today, where companies are coming under increasing pressure to shorten the time it takes to get products manufactured and into the market – to speed up the supply chain.

In order to address this, shop floor control systems such as Manufacturing Execution Systems (MES) track activity on the shop floor and provide information on variances to schedule in real time so that adjustments can be made where necessary. MRP II systems with planning horizons and fixed schedules do not provide for this type of flexibility.

In addition to MES for FCS systems, Distribution Resource Planning (DRP) systems provide functionality that enables coordination between the supply chain and operations. Integration of MES and DRP systems can provide real time feedback from the supply chain so that production can be adjusted quickly to respond. Care must be taken though as we cannot lose sight of the over-arching process strategy that defines how inventory is planned, organized and controlled.

Diehl and Armstrong contend that because of the static nature of MRP II systems and the built in assumption that capacity, lot sizes and lead times are fixed it is less flexible in responding to changing demand. (Diehl & Armstrong, 2011) With the increased pressure of speed and optimizing the entire supply chain, being able to adjust batch sizes and affect available capacity and, in turn, lead time aid in addressing the issue of speed.

IBM has also developed simulation software that operates similarly to how MRP II does, only in reverse. Based on what materials and components are in inventory and the number of end products it has to manufacture, the software simulates what their optimum supply chain should look like. It evolved from the need at IBM to short the time it took for demand forecasts to get into the hands of planners.

(Bartholomew, 1997) By pushing the component level data up, companies with complex supply chains can gain visibility on what the available resources are capable of supplying and make adjustments within the supply chain to meet demand forecasts. This data can then be fed into traditional planning systems such as MRP II or MES systems.

Conclusion

MRP II systems are ideal for structured decisions. Many manufacturing processes lend themselves to these types of systems; as was demonstrated, many inventory and production related problems are linear programming type problems, albeit complex ones. Where MRP II falls down is when the decisions aren't structured, where different steps need to be taken based on the product or process. For large, complex organizations where time is more critical, to maintain competitive advantage they have been shifting their focus to their supply chain. Variables traditionally fixed in MRP II systems such as batch size and lead times for them need to be dynamic.   For others, the demand forecasting process is slow and cumbersome and information can often be obsolete by the time it gets in the hands of planners. These types of issues bring to light that there is no "one size fits all" production planning system. Critical to successful planning system implementations is how inventory is managed and controlled, the nature of the product and market and demand patterns. As market dynamics and competitive environments within which firms operate evolve, as will information system requirements and functionality. Given that forecast demand is such a critical variable in production planning the ability to dynamically track forecast error, makes recommendations on forecasting approaches based on changing trends in the data and adjust forecasts accordingly may improve timeliness and accuracy in planning for those organizations with time sensitive supply chains of otherwise require that level of sophistication .

References

APICS The Association for Operations Management. (2010). *APICS Dictionary* (13th ed.). Chicago: APICS The Association for Operations Management.

APICS The Association for Operations Management. (2011). *APICS Operations Management Body of Knowledge* (3rd ed.). Chicago, Illinois: APICS The Association of Operations Management.

Arnold, J. T., & Chapman, S. N. (2004). *Introduction to Materials Management* (5th ed.). Upper Saddle River, New Jersey: Pearson Education Inc.

Bartholomew, D. (1997, July 21). MRP II in Reverse. *Industry Week, 246*(14), pp. 42-44.

Chase, R. B., Shankar, R., Jacobs, F. R., & Aquilano, N. J. (2011). *Operations & Supply Management* (12th ed.). New Delhi: Tata McGraw Hill Education Private Limited.

Diehl, G. W., & Armstrong, A. J. (2011, November). Marking MRP Work. *Industrial Engineer, 43*(11), pp. 35-40.

Frazell, E. H. (New York). *World-Class Warehousing and Material Handling.* 2002: McGraw-Hill.

Gumaer, R. (1996, September). Beyond ERP and MRP II. *IIE Solutions, 28*(9), pp. 32-35.

Heizer, J., & Render, B. (2006). *Operations Management* (8th ed.). Upper Saddle, New Jersey: Pearson Education Inc.

Hugos, M. (2006). *Essentials of Supply Chain Management.* Hoboken, New Jersey: John Wiley and Sons, Inc.

Janakiraman, V. S., & Sarukesi, K. (2009). *Decision Support Systems.* New Dehli: PHI Learning Private Limited.

Lofti, V., & Pegels, C. C. (1996). *Decision Support Systems for Operations Management & Management Science* (3rd ed.). Chicago: Richard D. Irwin.

Marakas, G. M. (2007). *Decision Support Systems In the 21st Century* (2nd ed.). New Delhi: Prentice-Hall of India.

SAP. (n.d.). *Form-Fit-Function (FFF Class).* Retrieved November 29, 2012, from SAP Help Portal: http://help.sap.com/saphelp_di46c2/helpdata/en/08/a111064d7611d2b438006094b9c9be/content.htm

Sauter, V. (1997). *Decision Support Systems: An Applied Managerial Approach.* New York: John Wiley and Sons, Inc.

www.ingramcontent.com/pod-product-compliance
Lightning Source LLC
Chambersburg PA
CBHW060523090326
40690CB00068BA/4362